A  BOOK

SPENDING MONEY

BUDGETS, CREDIT CARDS, SCAMS... AND MUCH MORE!

Jessica Cohn

Children's Press®
An imprint of Scholastic Inc.

Content Consultant
Dr. Marie A. Bussing
Emeriti Faculty, Romain College of Business
University of Southern Indiana

Library of Congress Cataloging-in-Publication Data
Names: Cohn, Jessica, author.
Title: Spending money: budgets, credit cards, scams . . . and much more! / by Jessica Cohn.
Description: First edition. | New York, NY: Scholastic, Inc., 2024. | Series: A true book: money! | Includes
    bibliographical references and index. | Audience: Ages 8–10. | Audience: Grades 4–6. | Summary: "A
    series to build strong financial habits early on in life! How can I make money? What is inflation? What
    is the difference between a debit card and a credit card? Economics—and more specifically, money—
    play such a large role in our lives. Yet there are many mysteries and misconceptions surrounding the
    basic concepts of finance and smart money management. This A True Book series offers students
    the know-how they'll need to start on the road to financial literacy—a crucial skill for today's world.
    Interesting information is presented in a fun, friendly way—and in the simplest terms possible—which
    will enable students to build strong financial habits early on in life. Understanding how to make a
    budget, how credit cards work, and how to avoid scams are just three critical financial literacy skills
    that all kids should have. Did you know that the first credit card was introduced in 1950? Or that
    American consumers lost more than $5 billion to frauds in 2021? Learn all this and more in Spending
    Money—a book that gives kids the confidence and know-how they need to manage their finances."—
    Provided by publisher.
Identifiers: LCCN 2022054133 (print) | LCCN 2022054134 (ebook) | ISBN 9781339004938 (library binding) |
    ISBN 9781339004945 (paperback) | ISBN 9781339004952 (ebk)
Subjects: LCSH: Money—Juvenile literature. | Budget—Juvenile literature. | Finance, Personal—Juvenile
    literature. | Credit cards—Juvenile literature. | BISAC: JUVENILE NONFICTION / Concepts / Money |
    JUVENILE NONFICTION / General
Classification: LCC HG221.5 .C64 2023 (print) | LCC HG221.5 (ebook) | DDC 332.024—dc23/eng/20221207
LC record available at https://lccn.loc.gov/2022054133
LC ebook record available at https://lccn.loc.gov/2022054134

10 9 8 7 6 5 4 3 2 1   24 25 26 27 28

Printed in China 62
First edition, 2024

Design by Kathleen Petelinsek
Series produced by Spooky Cheetah Press

Find the Truth!

Everything you are about to read is true *except* for one of the sentences on this page.

Which one is **TRUE**?

T or F "Phishing" is when someone borrows money and does not give it back.

T or F The main parts of a personal budget are income, expenses, and savings.

Find the answers in this book.

What's in This Book?

A budget helps families manage their spending.

Some people don't like to keep a lot of cash on hand.

Smart buyers weigh their choices before making a purchase.

INTRODUCTION

Think about what money can buy. Money pays for products, such as new shoes. It buys experiences, like going to the movies. **Any money you hold represents a series of decisions.** Should you spend that money or save it? And if you decide to spend the money, what is the smartest way to do that? Most people find it easy to spend money. But managing money so it does not run out takes more thinking and effort. **Managing spending is a skill.** And—as with any skill— you learn how it's done and keep practicing until you get better at it!

Governments spend money too. In 2022, U.S. government spending was 6.27 trillion dollars.

On average, a U.S. family spends more than $6,000 a year on entertainment, like going to see a movie.

Our Shared Economy

When you decide to spend money, your decision affects others. Your purchases are part of our **economy**—or how people produce, buy, and sell things. For example, if you find a snack you like and keep buying it, your grocer may stock more. If other stores do too, the snack company may hire more workers. One thing leads to another. Local economies feed into our country's economy, and that feeds into the world's economy—an exchange made up of billions of smaller exchanges.

Around the world, people buy more than 80 billion new clothing items each year.

Consumers in Action

We spend cash and other forms of money in exchange for goods and services. Goods are usually objects we can hold and use, such as backpacks and hats. Services are actions someone does for someone else. A lot of people have jobs where they provide a service. That includes movie directors, doctors, teachers, haircutters, coaches, and more.

When spending money on products or services for your own use, you act as a consumer. Smart consumers compare the price and quality of their options before spending.

Choices Consumers Make

The U.S. government keeps track of how much money American consumers spend each year. The chart shows how the average amount spent per consumer ($38,852*) was spread out among seven different categories. Americans spent the most on groceries. They spent the least on personal care, which includes things like cosmetics, hair products, and bath products.

*This amount does not include housing and health care.

Entertainment:
17%

Groceries
eaten at home:
25%

Gasoline and
other fuels:
10%

Food away
from home:
14%

Buying cars or
other vehicles:
23%

Things to wear and related
services: 8%

Products for personal care
and related services: 4%

Why Needs Come First

Families have to weigh both needs and wants when spending money. Needs are what we require to stay healthy, such as food, shelter, and clothing. Wants are enjoyable but not necessary, like taking big trips. If families spend money on all the things they want, there may not be enough left for their needs.

With each spending decision, you can ask yourself whether you need or want the purchase. Pay for what you need first. What you want today may not seem so important a month from now.

People often talk about how much money they save when they buy something on sale. Yet they are still spending money—often on something they don't really need. What point is the sale sign making?

© Mike Bald
B

SAVE UP TO 100%*
*WHEN YOU DON'T BUY ANYTHING

SALE!

Spending on one thing means the money is not available for something else. This cause and effect is known as opportunity cost.

Clearance
WAS: NOW $9⁹⁸

The store has more of these products than consumers want, so the store's managers have lowered the price.

Supply, Demand, and Your Spending

It can be hard to understand why some things cost so much. But the economy works in ways that determine prices. If there is a lot of one product available but not many people want it, the price for that product goes down. On the other hand, if there is a limited supply and a lot of people want the product, the price goes up. The supply of something and the demand for it affect each other. That is one reason why it is good not to spend money on impulse, or without much thought. The price may go down if you wait.

Financial literacy is understanding words and ideas about money management.

Families are not the only people who budget. Companies and countries have budgets too.

Managing Spending

A budget is a tool that examines spending—and helps people make better decisions. A household budget helps a family. A personal budget can help you organize your own funds. The three main parts of a budget are income, expenses, and savings. Income is money that comes in. Expenses are what you spend money on. Money left over builds savings for the future. Reviewing each spending decision listed in your budget can help you learn how to cut costs.

In the United States, about 61 percent of kids are given a weekly allowance. Most are expected to do work around the house in exchange.

Budgets cover both short-term spending goals, like buying someone a gift, and long-term goals, like paying for college.

Spending Limits

You can make a simple budget on paper. Start by listing and adding up your income, including payments for chores, birthday money, and your allowance, if you have one. By tracking the money coming in, you can better understand how much you have available to spend. You can see your spending limits. Knowing what you can afford is one key to managing spending. Once income is added up, the next step is to examine expenses.

Extra Expenses: Tax and Shipping

Have you ever spent money on sports equipment or another item and felt surprised by the final cost? That can happen after sales tax is added. To work out a final cost, multiply the price of the item by the sales tax where you live. If tax is 6 percent, and the price of the item is $10, the total cost will be $10.60 ($10 x .06 = 60¢ tax). In addition, if you are making an online purchase, check whether you must pay for shipping. Both taxes and shipping need to get figured in when budgeting for a purchase.

Groceries are not taxed in many places, but bills for restaurant meals usually include taxes.

Each state has its own sales tax rate. Many local governments add taxes too.

Saving on Your Spending

Monthly bills, like those for rent or heat, are a big part of household expenses. Statements for these bills show how much is owed for these ongoing, or fixed, expenses.

A family has more control over other kinds of expenses, such as how much they spend on food and entertainment. People can cut back on spending by choosing to go to a park instead of an arcade. They can use coupons, which offer discounts on groceries and other purchases.

Using coupons when you shop can lead to great savings.

YOUR ONLINE STORE

DISCOUNT COUPON
70% OFF
CLICK HERE NOW

MY SHOES STORE
Black high heel shoes

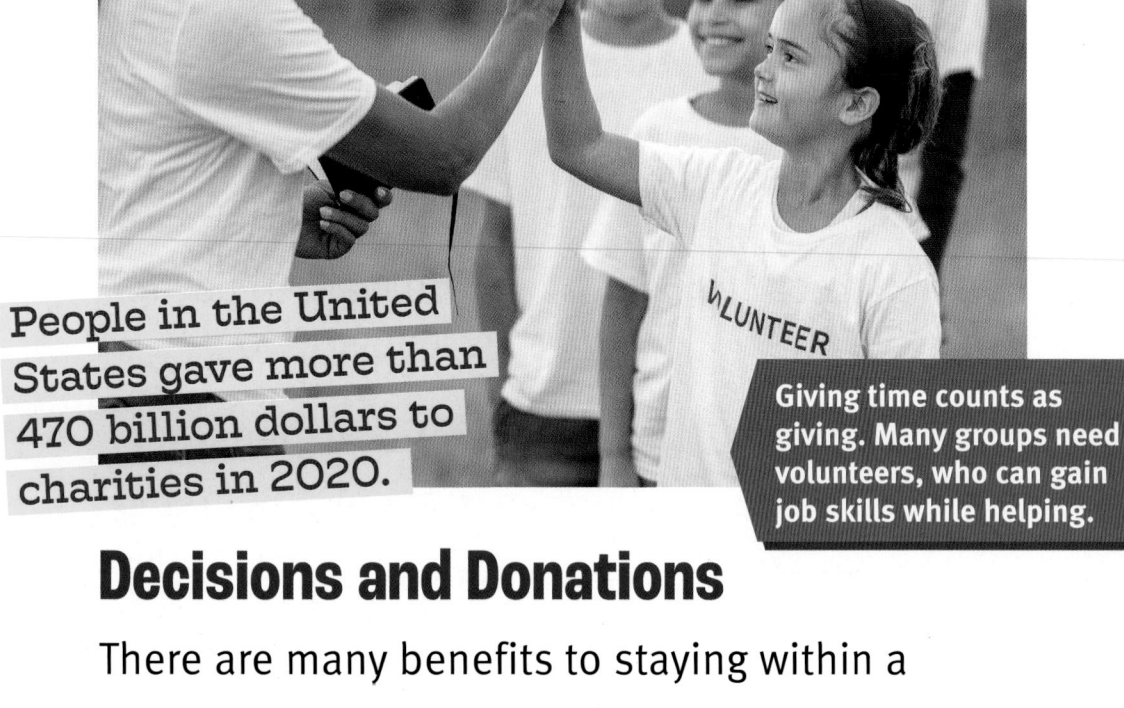

People in the United States gave more than 470 billion dollars to charities in 2020.

Giving time counts as giving. Many groups need volunteers, who can gain job skills while helping.

Decisions and Donations

There are many benefits to staying within a budget and cutting expenses. By cutting costs, you may have money left that you can spend on causes you care about. You can give some of that money to a charitable organization, such as an animal rescue group or a food bank.

Some people budget a certain amount to charity each month. Others give when they can. Even if there's no money in the budget for charities, you can donate your time!

Spending for Your Future

Any money left over after you subtract your expenses can be saved. By building savings, you can put money toward things you want to pay for in the future, like a bike or a school trip. You can also be better prepared for surprise expenses.

Have you heard the expression "saving for a rainy day"? That saying means it makes sense to plan for unexpected expenses. One common goal is to budget 15 to 20 percent of income for this purpose.

To balance a budget, money coming in needs to be equal to or greater than money spent. Consider what the character is saying. Has she made sure to cover their needs in the budget?

"So far, so good — I've got our budget all balanced except for food, clothing, and shelter!"

Make a Budget

Once you are ready to make your own budget, you can follow the example shown here. This is a budget for a student who gets an allowance of $10 per week. As you work on your own budget, keep this basic formula in mind: **INCOME − EXPENSES = SAVINGS**.

MONTHLY BUDGET

INCOME		EXPENSES	
WEEK 1	$ 10.00	$ 5.00	LUNCH
WEEK 2	$ 10.00	$ 3.00	SNACKS
WEEK 3	$ 10.00	$ 10.00	MOVIES
WEEK 4	$ 10.00	$ 6.00	BOOK
TOTAL	$ 40.00	TOTAL $ 24.00	

SAVINGS $16.00

A budget can show why you need to make sacrifices sometimes. You give up some of your wants to pay for your present and future needs.

In 2022, 41 percent of people in the United States said they typically do not pay cash for their purchases.

One advantage to opening a bank account is that the bank keeps a record of your spending.

Paying for What You Need

Some people do not like to carry cash around—especially if they are planning on making a big purchase. If you **deposit** your money in a bank account, you will have other spending options. In the United States, you must be at least 18 years old to open a bank account on your own. But many banks offer accounts specifically for young people that are set up and managed by a parent or guardian.

On Your Account

Some bank accounts come with a **debit card**. When you buy something with a debit card, the money is taken directly from your account. Or you can use the card to take cash from an automated teller machine (ATM). In both cases, you can spend only the amount of money that is in your account. If your account **balance** drops to zero, you will not be able to use the card.

A debit card's owner usually has to type in a personal identification number, or PIN, associated with the card to get money. People create their own PINs.

A teller is a person who helps customers inside banks. ATMs are computers that perform many of the same services.

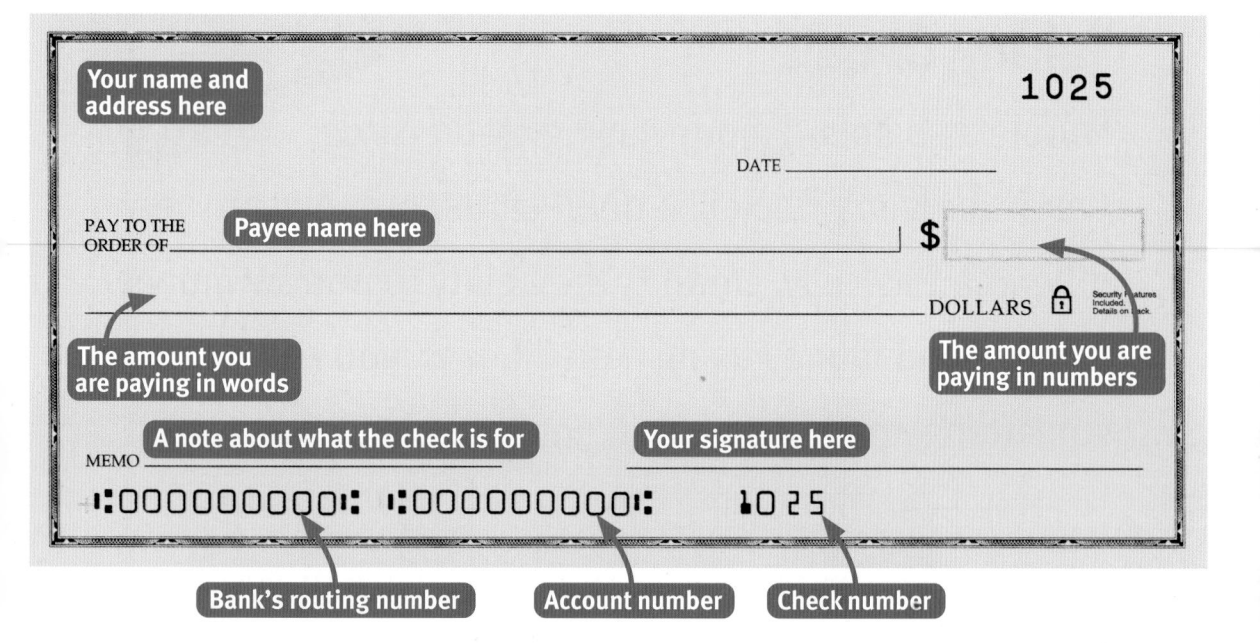

Your name and address here

1025

DATE _____

PAY TO THE ORDER OF _____ Payee name here _____ $ [   ]

_____ DOLLARS 🔒 Security Features Included. Details on back.

The amount you are paying in words

The amount you are paying in numbers

A note about what the check is for

Your signature here

MEMO _____ _____

⑆000000000⑆ ⑆000000000⑆ ⑈1025

Bank's routing number

Account number

Check number

Check It Out

Besides debit cards, checking accounts have another payment option, called a check. A check is a paper document that has your name and bank account number on it. Each check has a spot to write the name of the person or business you are paying (payee) and spots for the amount you are paying. Each check is like a promise that your bank will pay the payee the amount listed.

Taking Credit

People also spend money using credit cards. Credit cards may look like debit cards, but they are very different. Basically, credit is the ability to borrow money. If you spend money using a credit card, you can buy something and not pay for it until the bill arrives.

However, borrowing money and having **debt** is not free. When you use a credit card, you may need to pay **interest** on your purchase. The interest rate is a percentage of the total owed. It is a fee you pay to the bank or credit card company for the loan.

Timeline of Credit and Credit Cards

1800s
It is common for store owners to sell items on credit. They keep track of the charges in books.

1950
Diners Club issues the first modern credit card, which is made of thick paper. Cardholders pay the bill in full at the end of each month.

1958
Bank of America introduces BankAmericard, the first revolving credit card. That means the balance does not have to be paid each month.

26

Electronic Payments

Now more than ever, people spend and transfer money online. Many adults use **payment platforms** accessed by computers. The platforms allow users to easily exchange money while keeping account information safe.

Have you watched people wave their phones in front of card readers at a store? Many adults have payment systems with account information stored on their cell phones. They can use their phones instead of cards to pay bills or to make purchases.

1959
American Express makes the first plastic credit card. Other companies soon follow.

1968
Congress enacts the Truth in Lending Act. It requires that rules of credit be clearly stated and presented in a standard way.

2014
Apple Pay becomes the first payment system that people store on phones, eliminating the need to carry credit cards separately.

Spending on Spending?

Before using any account with any financial institution, it pays to know what fees you will be responsible for paying. For example, will you be charged if you take out money too often? What does the institution consider to be too often?

Banks often charge a monthly fee for maintaining an account. There can also be fees for using certain ATMs. And if people accidentally write a check for more money than they have in an account, they will likely have to pay an **overdraft** fee.

NOPE! I'M HOLDING ON TO YOUR MONEY UNTIL YOU AGREE TO MY $2 WITHDRAWAL FEE.

If you use an ATM that is not part of your bank's network, you may need to pay a fee. Based on what you know about banks, what does the piggy bank mean by a withdrawal fee?

In recent years, most of the purchases young people made online were related to game apps.

Keeping Track of Spending

Do you play games online or on your phone? Even when the games are free, they may have in-game purchases. If you do not pay attention, you can easily lose track of the money you spend this way. Make sure you look at your bank statement to track your spending and to balance your account. This monthly report shows all the money you deposited to your account. It also shows all the money that you took out. That includes, for example, checks you have written, ATM withdrawals, and payments made with your debit card. Subtract withdrawals from deposits to balance your account.

What Is the Cost of Credit?

Paying for something with a credit card is different from paying with cash, a check, or a debit card. A credit card company sends the bill on a certain day each month. You have a grace period, usually 25 to 55 days, to pay the money back. See what can happen if you do not pay!

DAY OF PURCHASE

You buy a $25 pair of shoes with a credit card. The cashier rings up $25 plus sales tax of 10 percent, or $2.50. The total is $27.50.

BILL ARRIVES

If you pay the full balance when the bill shows up, there will be no more fees. However, when the bill comes, you see a minimum payment listed. Companies have different minimums.

DECISION TIME

Imagine your minimum payment is 10 percent of the balance. For the shoes, it means you should pay at least $2.75.

· If you do not pay the minimum payment listed, you will be charged a late fee on top of what you owe.

· If you decide to make the minimum payment, you will still owe some money after that.

$$\$27.50 - \$2.75 = \$24.75$$

ONE MONTH LATER

APR stands for "annual percentage rate." That is a yearly rate charged for loans, but it is applied to your balance monthly. Imagine the APR for your card is 15 percent. That equals 1.25 percent per month.

$$.0125 \times \$24.75 = \$0.31$$
$$\$24.75 + \$0.31 = \$25.06$$

If you paid the minimum last month, this month you will owe $25.06.

$25.06 added to the $2.75 you already paid is $27.81. This is more than the original price of the shoes. And that number will continue to rise the longer you take to pay the credit card balance in full. Here is a tip for smart spending: If possible, use your credit card only if you will be able to pay the bill in full when it first arrives.

In 2021, scammers were able to steal more than 5.8 billion dollars from people in the United States.

Safe Spending

The key to managing money is to pay attention to your spending. But even people who are careful about how they spend money can end up losing lots of it. It is incredibly common for people—both young people and adults—to spend their money on **scams**.

A scam is a trick. Scammers may knock at the door. They may phone or send a letter. However, most young people who become victims of scams are targeted online. Knowing how to protect yourself against scams is an important part of money management.

Speech bubble: MOM SAYS IF YOU'RE GOING TO BUY ANYTHING ONLINE, I'M SUPPOSED TO MAKE SURE IT'S A SECURE SITE.

This cartoon is speaking to the fact that many kids are a lot more tech savvy than their parents! What will the kid look for to make sure the site is secure?

Online Shopping Scams

Many scammers operate fake shopping sites. When people pay for items, the scammers steal the money and do not send the items.

It is important to use secure sites when spending online. A secure URL starts with *https*, not *http*. The "s" stands for *secure* and shows that the site has a Secure Sockets Layer (SSL) certificate. Any information you give is encrypted, or coded, so no one else can read it. The site locks down account numbers, email addresses, and other key information.

Fake Charities

In another common scam, people pretend to be a charity. They might say they are helping victims of a natural disaster or collecting money for firefighters, police, or service members—but they keep the money for themselves. If a so-called charity wants cash, gift cards, or a wire transfer, do not deal with them. Real charities will ask for a donation by check or credit card. Online addresses for real charities usually end with *.org*. Beware when an address says *.com* at the end.

Do not give any personal information, such as your date of birth, to anyone who asks for a donation.

A group called Charity Watch keeps track of charities to help people identify fakes.

Avoid making purchases on public Wi-Fi that is not secure. People around you could steal your credit card numbers.

Most people in the United States get a Social Security number when they are born.

Identity Theft

Some scammers do not ask you to send money. They try to get access to your money instead. Identity theft happens when someone gets hold of data such as your bank account number or **Social Security number** and uses the information to pretend to be you. They spend your money or set up fake accounts in your name. It is important to guard your personal information carefully and to create secure passwords for your accounts.

Watch Out for Pop-Ups

Pop-ups are windows that appear on your screen without your permission. If you are searching online and a pop-up says you need to protect your computer from a virus, that's probably a trick to get access to your information. Pop-ups may also say that you have won a prize, are in legal trouble, or are locked out of accounts. No matter what, do not click on them. Pop-ups often contain a virus that allows scammers to read information on your computer or phone.

Scammers often also use social media, such as TikTok and Facebook. Do not click on links from unknown accounts.

If you get a suspicious message, share it with an adult.

Common Means of Contact

Some frauds are so common, they even have names! Learn the telltale signs of common kinds of fraud—and what you can do if targeted. Even if the sender seems familiar, you should ignore any requests from an unknown source.

WHAT IS THE SCAM?	WHAT TO DO
PHISHING: an email scam. Often, a phishing email will say your account has been "compromised."	Check for misspelled words or wrong contact information. This is usually a sign of a scam. Contact the company that supposedly sent the email to see if it has tried to make contact.
SMISHING: a scam by text. You may get a text that addresses you by name and gives you a link to click.	Don't click on the link. If you do, the scammer could get information off your phone. If a company's name is used, contact that company to report the scam.
PHARMING: fake shopping websites. Some scammers direct people to fake websites that look real but are not.	Look at the URL whenever you shop online. It should start with *https*, not *http*. Look for mistakes in spelling and for odd punctuation and capitalization. Those are clues that the site is fake.

Time Well Spent

Being smart about money starts with looking at your spending. Make a budget. Study your expenses. Set goals. You may find that you can get both what you need and what you want. You may find that you are even able to help causes you believe in.

If you practice the proven steps of budgeting and safeguard your spending, you can gradually feel more in control—and set even higher goals. With a realistic budget, you can save for the future and spend with a plan.

Studies show that people who stick to a budget report less stress.

Credit Scores

A credit score is a rating people can earn. People with large credit balances who are late paying their bills have low credit scores. People with small balances who pay their bills on time have high scores. Having a good credit score is important when you need to take out a loan or want to apply for a credit card. Here is a look at a range of possible scores.

Range of Credit Scores

Fair	580 to 669
Good	670 to 739
Very Good	740 to 799
Excellent	800 and up

Credit Score

Your Credit Score

810

EXCELLENT

Updated 5 days ago

YOU

BAD

EXCELLENT

It is good to know your credit score.

As you read on page 26, interest is a rate a borrower pays for a loan. This chart shows the average interest rates people with different credit scores get charged when they apply for a credit card. Use the data to answer the questions below.

Average Credit Card Interest Rates
(For all credit cards)
Fair credit score: 24%
Good credit score: 22%
Very good credit score: 17%
Excellent credit score: 16%

Analyze It!

1. What is the average credit card interest rate for someone with a credit score of 820?

2. What is the average credit card interest rate for someone with a credit score of 600?

3. What is the difference in interest rates for a person with fair credit and a person with excellent credit?

4. Why do you think people with an excellent credit score can get a better interest rate than those with a fair credit score?

ANSWERS: 1. 16%; **2.** 24%; **3.** Eight percentage points; **4.** People who have proven that they pay their bills are better candidates for a credit card. The company can have more confidence that they will be paid back.

Be a Smart Shopper!

Groceries make up a big part of most family budgets. About 90 percent of people use coupons when they shop—or they check sales flyers and adjust their shopping lists to include items that are on sale. Another way to save is through comparison shopping. This activity shows you how that works.

Materials

Marker or pen
Paper

Directions

1 Use a marker or pen to make a chart with four columns and at least 10 rows, like the one shown on the next page. In the first column, list food items you like to have at home.

2 Ask an adult to walk down the aisles of a grocery store with you so you can check prices. In the second column, write down the price of a name-brand product for each item on the list.

SHOPPING LIST

FOOD	NAME-BRAND PRICE	STORE-BRAND PRICE	SAVINGS

3 In the third column, write down the price of the store-brand product for the same item.

4 In the fourth column, note how much you can save by using the store brand.

5 Which products would you be able to save the most on? How much money could your family save every week by using store brands?

True Statistics*

Amount the average U.S. household spends on groceries each year: About $9,700

Amount the average U.S. household spends on entertainment each year: More than $6,000

Common weekly allowance for kids in the United States: $1 to $2 for each year of age

Average sales tax in the United States: 6 percent

Average age for first credit card in the United States: 18 to 20

Number of scams reported worldwide in 2020: 266 million

Note: These statistics are as of 2022.

Did you find the truth?

(F) "Phishing" is when someone borrows money and does not give it back.

(T) The main parts of a personal budget are income, expenses, and savings.

Resources

Other books in this series:

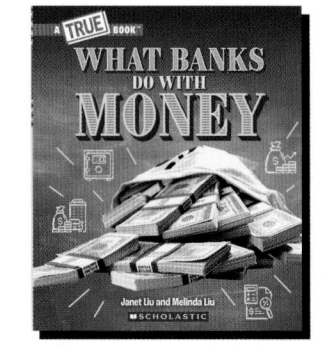

You can also look at:

Cribb, Joe. *Eyewitness: Money*. New York: Dorling Kindersley, 2016.

McGillian, Jamie Kyle. *The Kids' Money Book: Earning, Saving, Spending, Investing, Donating*. New York: Union Square Kids, 2016.

Sember, Brette McWhorter. *The Everything Kids' Money Book: Earn It, Save It, and Watch It Grow!* Avon, MA: Adams Media, 2008.

Glossary

balance (BAL-uhns) the amount a customer has in a checking or savings account or that they owe on a credit card

debit card (DEB-it KAHRD) a plastic card that is connected to a bank account and that can be used to pay for things

debt (DET) money that someone owes

deposit (di-PAH-zit) to put money into a bank account

economy (i-KAH-nuh-mee) the system of buying, selling, making things, and managing money in a place

financial (fye-NAN-shuhl) having to do with the management and use of money by businesses, banks, and governments

interest (IN-trist) a fee paid for borrowing money, usually a percentage of the amount borrowed, as well as money paid to you by a bank for keeping your savings there

overdraft (OH-vur-draft) when a person takes more out of their bank account than they had on deposit

payment platforms (PAY-mint PLAT-formz) systems that read payment cards and send data to and from a customer account

scams (SKAMZ) deceptive acts

Social Security number (SOH-shuhl si-KYOOR-i-tee NUHM-bur) number assigned to people in the United States for identification

Index

Page numbers in **bold** indicate illustrations.

About the Author

When she was young, Jessica Cohn saved all her money in a box under her bed until her mother took her to the bank, two blocks away, where she opened her first savings account. Cohn has written more than 60 nonfiction books. She has a master of science in Written Communications and decades of editing experience. For a podcast that helps students learn even more about money, Cohn recommends *Million Bazillion*, produced by American Public Media.